It's

IVOR DAVIES

Foulis

Haynes
®

ISBN 0 85429 786 3

© Ivor Davies 1990

First published May 1990

A FOULIS Motorcycling Book

Published by:
Haynes Publishing Group
Sparkford, Nr. Yeovil, Somerset BA22 7JJ, England

Haynes Publications Inc
861 Lawrence Drive, Newbury Park, California 91320 USA

British Library Cataloguing in Publication Data
Davies, Ivor, *1913 –*
It's easy on a Triumph.
1. Motorcycles, history
I. Title
629.2'275'09

ISBN 0-85429-786-3

Library of Congress Catalog Card No: 89-81728

Editor: Jeff Clew

Printed in England by J.H. Haynes & Co. ltd.

CONTENTS

INTRODUCTION
and ACKNOWLEDGEMENTS

This is a book about motorcyclists rather than motorcycles. The title comes from a series of advertisements by Alex Oxley which Triumph put out from Meriden in the post-war period, some of which are reproduced on later pages. This was when motorcycles were in very short supply due mainly to a lack of materials following the war. It took a long time to get back to normal and also for the factory to gear itself up for peacetime production. In the meantime the customers were anxiously waiting for their new Speed Twins and Tiger 100s. We felt obliged to advertise in the two weekly magazines in order a) to ensure that *they* didn't go out of business, they were vital to the development of the trade and sport and b) remind our customers that we were making civilian motorcycles again.

I am not quite sure who thought up the tag "It's Easy on a Triumph" – I suspect it was Alex Oxley himself. He came up with suggestions for a number of crazy situations and we suggested others for him to draw. The basic idea behind the series was to avoid doing a "hard-sell" on Triumph. The customer must not be persuaded to dash off hotfoot to his dealer, chequebook in hand, which was the job of a normal advertisement. He should just be reminded that Triumph was still very much around and, hopefully, the humour would leave him thinking kindly of us.

This book illustrates a large number of Triumph riders of the period, taking part in various hazardous occupations like road racing, trials riding, scrambling, trick riding, record breaking, riding round the world and so on, the inference being, would you believe, that – "It's Easy on a Triumph."

See what *you* think!

I offer my apologies to those copyright holders of some of the older photographs where all efforts to contact them have failed. I would like to record my sincere thanks to Ralph Venables for identifying photographs, to Edward (Ed) Stott for ISDT results, to Ken Heanes for information on the ISDT in the USA, to Henry Vale for trials reminiscences over a cup of tea, to Anthony Smith for details and pictures of his journeys, to John Hancox for his drawings, to Les Williams for race programmes, to John Nelson for Daytona race details and Doug Hele for the photographs, and to my son John for some clever photography. A final 'thank you' to one of our old colleagues, Don Brown of California, for information on American photographs.

Finally I hope that the series of anecdotes entitled "Meriden Moments" will raise a smile. Meriden was that sort of place, something was always happening and the result was often a good laugh. If any of you out there can recall other "Meriden Moments" (and I am sure you can) please let me have them so that we can add to the collection.

Kenilworth
April 1989

ON THE TRACK

The attitude of the Triumph company to racing has varied over the years depending on the situation at the time. In the very early days of the motorcycle it was necessary to demonstrate the speed and particularly the reliability of the products that you sold to your customers. The Tourist Trophy races in the Isle of Man were started for this purpose, hence the inclusion of the word "Tourist" in the title. Triumph were in at the start and came 2nd and 3rd in the very first single cylinder class race in 1907, with one retirement. The following year Triumph collected 1st, 3rd, 4th, 5th, 7th and 10th places with just one retirement. The "Trusty Triumph" nickname must have started around this time.

Support between the wars for the TT was very lukewarm, a 2nd place in 1922 and 3rd in 1927 being the only results of any note. After the Second World War the cat was put well and truly among the pigeons when Ernie Lyons on a Tiger 100, quietly prepared by Freddie Clarke of Brooklands fame, won the 1946 Manx Grand Prix. This led to the introduction of the "Grand Prix" model which won again in 1948. It was never intended as a serious competitor to the Manx Norton but as a bike on which the club rider could compete satisfactorily at club level without bankrupting himself.

I have explained Edward Turner's views on racing many times before. He was entirely opposed to factories producing exotic machinery which bore no resemblance whatever to the showroom product apart from the name on the tank. Designing and building these, he said, diverted the money and best brains of a company away from making the best possible products for sale to the customer whose money kept the company in business. He was not against the racing of production motorcycles as the Triumph record in this category proved, later on.

VICTORIES AT DAYTONA

After Turner the situation changed somewhat when Harry Sturgeon took over. The American market was vital to Triumph and in 1965 it was agreed that to maintain our sales momentum over there something really sensational was needed – like a major road racing success. The Daytona 200 Mile Experts Race was **THE** event of the year in America and Meriden decided to have a crack at it with the co-operation of our American companies.

The racing Tiger 100 was the only really competitive 500 in the group and a big programme of improvements was launched to give it a chance against the combined might of the American and Oriental opposition. Doug Hele was the mastermind in charge and he was given a free hand by Sturgeon to do whatever was necessary. Doug was no stranger to the racing scene having been heavily involved at Bracebridge Street when Nortons were in full flight and winning everything.

Full details of the work done and of the race can be found in John Nelson's book *Triumph Tiger 100/Daytona* (Haynes) and a very absorbing story it is too. It had a very happy ending as the outcome was a decisive victory for Triumph not only in 1966 but 1967 as well!

To illustrate this section I have selected a variety of good racing shots at various venues and on various models from Cub to Trident. I had difficulty in captioning some of these as photographers rarely put anything on their prints and when these are 20 or 30 years old, this does present a problem. Identifying the rider is not difficult but the date and location is another matter. However, I have done quite well, aided by Les Williams, owner of 'Slippery Sam', who has a good memory when it comes to racing.

MERIDEN MOMENTS

No 1 WEATHERLINE

Harry Summers was a senior draughtsman and designer at the Triumph factory at Meriden and his gifted pencil had decreed the shape of many components on a whole range of Triumph models over the years. Wishing to report to the Managing Director, Edward Turner, on an item the latter had queried earlier that day, he picked up his internal phone and depressed the hallowed No 1 key. ET came on the other end. "Summers here sir," said Harry. The Managing Director looked out of his office window where a cloudburst was in progress, the rain streaming down the glass. "You could have fooled me," he growled.

No 2 ROUND THE WORLD IN 80 SECONDS !

Potential round-the-world travellers on motorcycles were a constant pain to busy factories, the Triumph works at Meriden being no exception. They would turn up out of the blue, all starry-eyed, to explain the colossal publicity which would rebound to the factory's benefit if a) We gave them a bike. b)We provided a wide range of spare parts, f.o.c. of course. c) We guaranteed to rescue them every time they got bogged down in some Bolivian backwater.

It was my painful duty as Publicity Manager to explain the facts of life to these aspiring adventurers. The costs involved in providing items a), b), and c) described above would more than cancel out the minimal amount of publicity likely to be obtained even if the trip was successful, which was unlikely.

There was just one exception to this routine scenario; his name was Ted Simon. We did lend him a bike and he did ride around the world, *but* he was sponsored by a leading Sunday national newspaper who did print his adventures from time to time and on his return, he wrote two splendid books.

However this story really concerns another enthusiast with world touring ambitions. I think he came from Canada or South Africa. He arrived at the works to collect his repaired Thunderbird, climbed on and kicked it up. Waving farewell to the mechanics, he roared down the exit road from the factory, straight across the traffic laden A45 highway, over the grass verge and through the hedge!

It transpired that his experience of riding powerful motorcycles was strictly limited.

Below: A dramatic picture of Welshman Malcolm Uphill and his Triumph Bonneville on their way to winning the 1969 Production TT in the Isle of Man at 99.99 mph with a record lap at 100.37 mph, the first time that a production bike had lapped the Island at over 100 mph. An 8ft wide print of this picture is displayed on a wall of the National Motorcycle Museum near Birmingham.

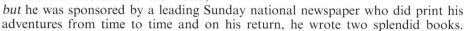

Left: Bob (Fearless) Foster on one of six GP Triumphs in the 1948 Senior TT, seen here on the Mountain. Regrettably all six retired! In 1949 7 finished, 6 retired. In 1950 6 finished, 3 retired. Triumph did better in the Manx GP, winning in 1946 and 1948.

Right: Don Crossley (GP Triumph) winner of the 1948 Senior Manx Grand Prix. He seems to be worried about something at the back end of his machine but it could not have been serious seeing that he went on to win.

Below: Bernard Hargreaves squeezing the last ounce out of his Tiger 100 heads for a win in the 1952 Clubmans TT at 82.45 mph. The bike looks very standard except that someone has purloined the dynamo from between the front engine plates! Every ounce saved helps a little.

Above: I could not find a photograph of Ernie Nott on a Triumph but this shot of him on a works Husqvarna, probably the 350 on which he finished 3rd in the 1934 Junior TT, is a splendid substitute. As I have said on another page Ernie was the "greatest TT rider never to have won a TT". He rode works Rudges from 1927 to the mid-thirties and achieved fame by being the first man to cover 200 miles in 2 hours (on a 500 Rudge). After the war he joined his old Rudge team mate, Tyrell Smith to help run the Experimental Department at Meriden.

Left: Norman Hyde blasting away on his 831cc Trident-engined outfit. He is currently holder of the World sidecar speed record at 161.8 mph. He has also set many other World and British short distance records, always Triumph mounted. At Meriden he was the engineer in charge of three cylinder development and Doug Hele's assistant on the works racers. He now runs his own business in Warwick specialising in Triumph parts including many Hyde-designed high performance products.

Tony Jefferies on his works Trident set a scorching pace to win the new 750cc Formula race in the Isle of Man in 1971. He averaged 102.85 mph and finished 26 seconds ahead of the favourite, Ray Pickrell (BSA Rocket 3).

Mick Grant sweeping round the Silverstone curves on a production Trident owned and prepared by Stan Shenton, the well-known London Triumph dealer. Mick was the winner of the 1974 Production TT on the celebrated "Slippery Sam".

Another Silverstone shot, this time of John Cooper being hotly pursued by Meriden's own Percy Tait. Who crossed the line first is not known but both being on triples there was probably not much in it.

A relaxed picture of Percy Tait, Trident mounted, taken during the Hutchinson 100 at Brands Hatch in 1972. Percy's job at Meriden was testing everything new that was produced and this involved very high mileages, day after day. In his spare time he went racing – just for a change!

Koelliker was the name of the Triumph distributor in Milan, Italy – they also handled Jaguar (only the best!). They ran a full blown race shop complete with test beds and a team of very quick Tridents. Their star rider was Gianfranco Bonera who is here seen cranked over somewhere near the limit.

A Brands Hatch shot of Ray Pickrell in the Hutchinson 100 held in August 1972. Two months before, in the Isle of Man, Ray had won both the Production TT (at 100.00 mph) and the Formula 750 TT (at 104.23 mph) riding works Tridents of course. In the latter race, Tony Jefferies, also on a Trident, finished second, just 48 seconds behind.

Percy Tait winning again, this time at Silverstone in 1973 riding the incredible "Slippery Sam", the Trident that won the Isle of Man Production TT race five years in succession – from 1971 to 1975. No other single machine has ever done this in the long history of the TT – and is unlikely to do so again in the future.

Ray Pickrell again, a close-up this time, in the 1972 Hutchinson 100 at Brands Hatch. A real stylist, Ray looks completely at ease yet is motoring as hard as he can, which usually means that the opposition is left well and truly behind.

A classic shot of Tony Jefferies almost scraping Silverstone's tarmac. In Production and Formula 750 races in the Isle of Man during the years 1971/73 Tony scored two wins, two second places and one third, all on Tridents.

D.G. Harrison really getting down to it in the 1949 Port Elizabeth 200. He was GP mounted and finished second at 88 mph. The winner was C. B. Groves on another GP.

Shelsley Walsh Hill Climb. This famous event which is one of the classics in the car world was rudely invaded by a motorcyclist on 5th October 1946. The invader was Ernie Lyons, fresh from his sensational victory in the Manx Grand Prix a month earlier. Riding his Freddie Clarke-prepared 500cc Triumph he coolly proceeded to put up the fastest time of the day on two wheels or four! Here he motors round the notorious "S" bend on his way to the top.

Lyons Dinner. We had organised a dinner at the Bath Hotel in Leamington Spa (now gone) to celebrate Ernie's victory in the Isle of Man and quite by chance this was on the same day as Shelsley. So, happily, as it turned out, we were able to celebrate two famous victories. Ernie's schedule was so tight that he arrived in Leamington just in time and had to sit the dinner out still in his leathers! Here he is saying a few words. The solid row of smokers would not be popular today.

The Triumph Club of Vienna was (and possibly still is) a very flourishing and enthusiastic band of Triumph owners who came to Meriden from time to time in gleaming black leathers on glittering motorcycles. Their leader was Hans Bahmer, an arch enthusiast, seen here in a local (Austrian) hill climb. He rides a Bonnie and finished 3rd in the Over 500cc class.

Bobby Turner flat out on the beach at Daytona – no one could get flatter than that!

An unidentified American flat track rider – looks as if he is about to take a big handful of throttle.

Below: Another unidentified American in an hurry. The bike is easily identified as an early (plunger) Terrier or Cub.

Right: The winner of the 1958 Catalina Grand Prix crosses the line to an enthusiastic wave of the chequered flag. The rider was Bob Sandgren and the bike a Triumph TR6. Sandgren is the only man to have won this event two years running – 1957 and 1958. He was a longshoreman, "big and physical (200lbs)" and was a consistent finisher in desert events of the era. Flag waver was Frank 'Red' Kennedy, an AMA official. The 100 miles

course, comprising tarmac and slippery fire roads climbing to 1400 feet, was covered in 3hrs 27mins 19secs. There were 200 competitors. Catalina Island is located 27 miles off the coast of California.

A shot of Buddy Elmore, winner of the 1966 Daytona Race, with his Tiger 100 on full song! Gary Nixon was the winning rider in 1967.

The 1966 Daytona Tiger 100 which was basically standard but carried many modifications to fit it for its task which was to win the race. This it did without missing a beat, a great tribute to the team that prepared it and to Buddy Elmore who rode it.

The 1967 Daytona winning Tiger 100 which had several significant changes from 1966 – the Fontana front brake, restyled fuel tank, seat and fairing.

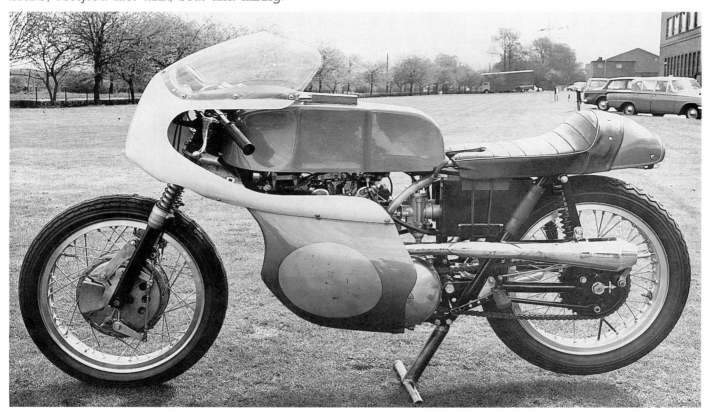

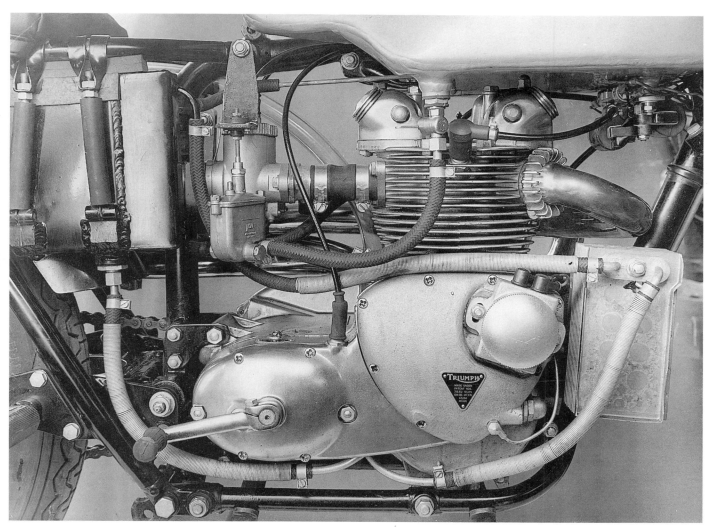

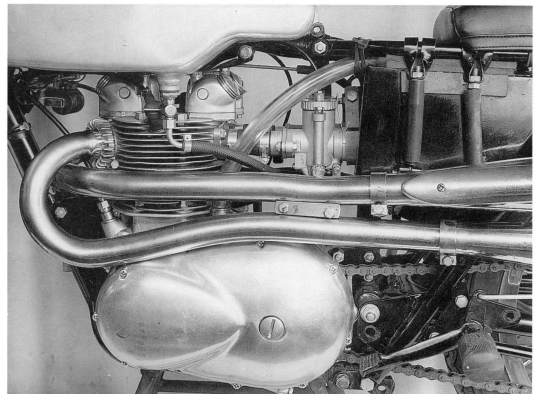

1966 Daytona winning T100 engine (Offside) Two $1\frac{1}{16}$ diameter Amal GP carburettors with remote rubber suspended racing float bowls. Oil cooler mounted forward of the engine. Elektron timing cover with exhaust camshaft driven Lucas racing contact breaker unit.

(Nearside) $1\frac{1}{2}$ in diameter exhaust pipes into reverse cone megaphones with 2in outlets. Short brake pedal adjacent to rear mounted footrest. Standard crankcase and primary chaincase.

In one of the "Meriden Moments" series I tell the story of the mysterious race-prepared Tiger 100 that found its way to the Isle of Man in 1955 unbeknown to most people in the works and particularly the Managing Director. It was revealed to him by an unthinking mechanic – but you read the story! This is a photograph of that T100, ridden by New Zealander M. E. Low who unfortunately retired. It looks a real beauty doesn't it?

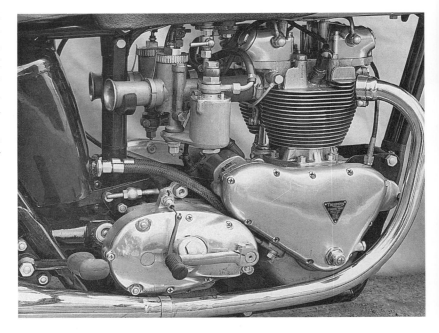

IT'S EASY ON A TRIUMPH

BREAKING RECORDS

Record breaking has been with us since the dawn of the powered two wheeler. The aim was always to get from 'A' to 'B' quicker than the last man or to go further than anyone else in one hour, two hours, three hours or whatever. Land's End to John O'Groats was a favourite challenge in the early days and was resurrected in 1963 in our 'Gaffers Gallop', but we were not out to break records on that occasion.

Triumph were not interested in record breaking until the Americans started blasting up and down the Bonneville Salt Flats at highly indecent speeds using our products. Johnny Allen was the first one. In 1955 his efforts resulted in Triumph becoming embroiled with the FIM over authenticity of the times recorded. Jess Thomas had a go, followed by Bill Johnson, whose record of 224 mph was courteously recognised by the FIM and we were at peace again. Bob Leppan clocked 245.6 mph but used two engines coupled together, the combined capacity putting him outside the FIM limit so no claim was made except in USA where it was 'legal'.

Finally, we had a 200cc Tiger Cub doing 150 mph which seems ridiculous – but is absolutely true!

JESS THOMAS, American record breaker, at speed on the Bonneville Salt Flats, Utah. On 28th August 1958 with a 500cc Triumph twin engine he clocked a 212.278 mph two direction average over the measured mile. With a 650cc engine on the same day he recorded 214.470 mph.

Right: In 1962 Bill Johnson, a 38 year old American truck driver, broke the World speed record for motorcycles with an average of 224.57 mph over a measured kilometre at Bonneville Salt Flats. His 17 foot cigar-shaped streamliner was built round a 650cc Triumph twin engine.

Main picture: In August 1966 Bob Leppan became the fastest man on two wheels with a speed of 245.6 mph, which was a new AMA record but did not count as a FIM World record because he used two 650cc Triumph engines coupled together, so exceeding the official capacity limit of 1000cc.

The man who started the streamliner cult – Texan Johnny Allen (centre). With a Triumph 650cc engine tucked away in the shell he achieved 193 mph in 1955 and 214 mph the following year. With him above are (left) Stormy Mangham, designer of the shell, and (right) Jack Wilson, who prepared the engine. Allen's machine can be seen in the National Motorcycle Museum, Birmingham, England together with many other racing Triumphs.

149 mph with a Tiger Cub!! On August 26th 1959 Bill Martin, Burbank, California Triumph dealer set a new AMA two-way record for 200cc machines of 139.82 mph over a measured mile. A one-way speed of 149.315 mph was achieved. Pictured above is Martin's streamliner, with Martin on the left. Preparation and tuning of the engine was done by Dale and Lonnie Martin, Bill Martin's sons, also in the picture.

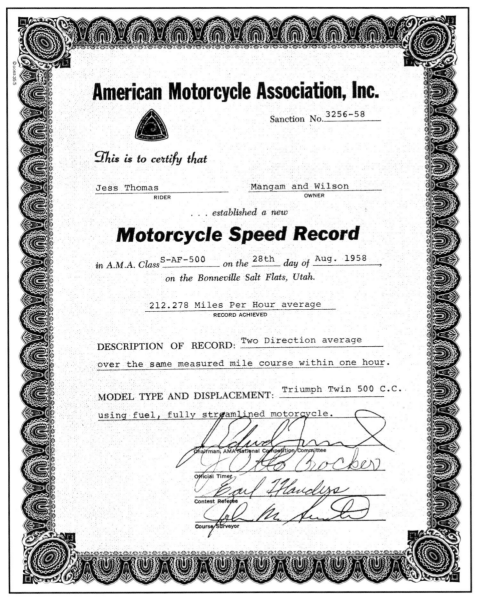

AMA CERTIFICATES

A small collection of American Motorcycle Association Certificates relating to records broken on the Bonneville Salt Flats by American Triumph riders in the fifties. These found their way to Meriden and sat undisturbed for a long time. I thought they might now be of interest.

Johnny Allen 25 Sept 1955 192.300 mph
Johnny Allen 6 Sept 1956 198.020 mph
Johnny Allen 6 Sept 1956 214.400 mph
Jess Thomas 28 Aug 1958 212.278 mph
Jess Thomas 28 Aug 1958 214.470 mph

A spectacular view of the Bonneville Salt Flats – with not a record breaking car or motorcycle in sight! The salt covers a total area of 200 square miles and is harvested annually for commercial purpose. (Photo courtesy GMWS, Salt Lake City).

No 3 TROUBLE WITH A TWIST GRIP!

When the Tina automatic scooter was introduced by Triumph in 1962 it was agreed that the marketing would have to be really professional because the Tina was going to be bought by the great British public – not by motorcyclists. The usual whole page advertisement in *The Motor Cycle* was quite the wrong approach. This had to be a London job so we sent for the pink – shirted experts from the West End. They were full of ideas (they always are – expensive ones!) and, in fact, we launched Tina at the London Festival Hall, an

event quite unprecedented in the parochial British motorcycle industry of the time. That was another story altogether, but for starters a deputation from the advertising agency arrived at the works to "evaluate" the product. They knew nothing about scooters or motorcycles but that was of no consequence they informed us – a product was a product was a product to them, whether it was a washing machine or a tin of dog food. They would soon have all the answers.

After it was explained how simple the Tina was to ride ("no gears, no clutch – goes at a touch" – my slogan!) the visitors were keen to have a go themselves. Unfortunately it was wet that day so we moved the demo into one of the big machine shops which had been temporarily emptied pending installation of new equipment.

After we had ridden round ourselves to show how it should be done, the first young man from London climbed on with a confident smile. He took off smoothly but half way down the shop, to our horror, he wound the twist grip wide open and the machine took off smartly. We closed our eyes as the end wall loomed up but at the last moment the rider stamped on the brake, the scooter slewed round and deposited him on the deck in a heap. After we had dusted him down and checked for broken bones, he explained that as all levers on bicycles pull towards you to stop he reckoned the twist grip should rotate towards you to shut off! Logical I suppose?

MOTORCYCLES AND THE MILITARY

The main role of the motorcycle in the forces was always the carrying of messages, orders and suchlike between formations and this critical task was done very efficiently – I know, I was a despatch rider once! However, with the development of radio, the motorcyclist as a message carrier was reduced to taking awkward packages, maps etc which could not go by radio. Also it had always been reckoned that the motorcyclist could usually 'get through' where other vehicles could not, but with the advent of the Land Rover and other four wheel drive trucks even this advantage has been whittled away.

So what is left for the poor army motorcyclist? One prime job is escorting heavy loads, guns, tanks, convoys, where the two wheeler can nip on ahead and clear traffic or guard crossroads or even ascertain if the enemy is holding the next village (this can be rather hazardous!).

There is one job left which nothing else can do however and that is stunt riding in a regimental motorcycle display team. The Royal Signals have a display team that has been performing for over half a century (not the same one of course). When they started, horses were used in the performance as well as motorcycles because horses were a normal form of transport used by the army just as motorcycles and lorries were. Many other units have had display teams – the Royal Artillery and Royal Marines to name but two.

The Royal Signals team, or 'White Helmets' as they are known today, have used Triumphs right from the start and Meriden always appreciated the valuable publicity which resulted from the team's appearance in all parts of the world. Members of the team are presented with white helmets when judged proficient enough to take part in the displays.

This is a slightly more up-to-date shot where the bike, if not obscured by the smoke, can be seen to be a 350 ohv. These had tanks in Tiger colours but were really 3Ts.

These two pictures show team members having a try out on the lawn in front of the Triumph factory at Meriden. They had just collected their bikes after the usual winter overhaul. The date is 1964 and they are riding the 500cc twin cylinder side valve TRW designed specifically for the forces.

I make no excuse for publishing this picture once more (it was in *It's a Triumph*) as I have since come across a most interesting letter from Australia relating to this particular picture. It is reproduced overleaf.

Here is an interesting little picture that a friend of mine came up with recently. It shows him in his early army days as trumpeter H. J. Hewitt, 2nd Medium Regt. Royal Artillery at Fargo Camp, Larkhill; in 1932. His bike is a 1927 4.94 hp Triumph Type N de Luxe (to quote the catalogue). The engine was a single cylinder side-valve with aluminium piston and roller bearing big-end. The gearbox had 3 speeds and was hand controlled. With Lucas Magdyno electric lamps and bulb horn it cost, when new, just £52.15.0 (£52.75).

The Manager
Triumph Motor Cycle Co
Meriden Works
Coventry, England

NSW Australia 20-8-75

Dear Sir,
I enclose, as an item of possible interest, a reminiscence of mine which was included in a recent issue of the "Despatch" which is the bulletin of the NSW Military History Society.

It deals with my first motor bike, a World War 1 Model single cylinder, belt driven, hub geared, acetylene lighted Triumph, chase started and lubricated by a stroke of the oil pump plunger every ten miles.

I had more fun and pleasure from that old machine than with much later models of Harley-Davidson and other heavy monsters fitted with sophisticated accessories.

Even to this day a Triumph parked at the kerbside never fails to bring me to an admiring halt.

With my good wishes
Yours faithfully
"Bert E. Weston"

The rider later saw service with the Regiment as part of the BEF in 1939/40 and was evacuated from Dunkirk. Commissioned in 1942 he saw service in North Africa and Italy. He was demobilised in 1946 with the rank of Captain.

*THE "DON R"

In World War 1 the despatch riders in France were for the most part mounted on Douglas, Rudge and Triumph motorcycles. The latter machine, always advertised as the "Trusty Triumph", was during the war the subject of a drawing in the English magazine *Motor Cycling* which forever captured my schoolboy imagination.

It depicted a goggled 'Don R' crouched low over the handlebars of a Triumph in sloppy conditions on a battlefields road lined with pollarded trees and cornering at speed.

Shells were bursting in the fields on either side of him plus a couple overhead for good measure –the enemy gunners had him well bracketed – and rifle bullets were sending up splashes from road puddles near the front wheel.

The accompanying jingle ran:-
"It's a muddy road and a bloody road
And a road that's swept by fire
But we've got to get through with the orders bus
Or we'll rouse the C.O.'s ire
So you'll stick at the bend I know old girl
Stick it and not turn a hair
Just one more dash through one more splash
And we're there old girl, WE'RE THERE."
At war's end some of these machines came on the Australian market and in my early twenties
I became the proud owner of a 1914 3½hp single cylinder belt-driven Triumph of Flanders Fields vintage.

This faithful steed carried me to country dances and balls for miles around my South Coast home and often my ride home in the wee early hours and with the above verse in mind would see me tearing along under the setting moon, hunched low to present as small a target as possible. Fences became wire entanglements in No Man's Land, cattle in nearby paddocks were enemy troops, farmhouses were pill boxes and my dash through sleeping villages with wide open exhaust earned me many a decoration for cold blooded daring and valour.

Signals jargon for DR –Despatch Rider

MOTOR CYCLING.   December 22, 1955

IT'S EASY—

ON A
TRIUMPH
The Best Motorcycle in the World
TRIUMPH ENGINEERING CO., LTD., MERIDEN WORKS, ALLESLEY, COVENTRY

ESCORT BUSINESS

Triumph was in the escort business in quite a big way through its many police customers in all parts of the world. One of the problems was to tune and gear the bike to go slowly without overheating. The Metropolitan Police were very good at this as you would expect –most of the big events happened in London on their ''patch''.

There was a story often told in Meriden that just before the war the Metropolitan Police had invited all the leading manufacturers to submit motorcycles for test as they were about to invest in a new fleet. The Speed Twin was new and not ready at the start of this operation but Edward Turner arrived with the bike as the tests were almost concluded. He persuaded them to try the Speed Twin and it was put through its paces after all the others and came out on top! That was the start of the lasting relationship between Triumph and the Met who bought large numbers of motorcycles from us for many years.

This decision had a considerable effect on other forces and it was not long before a fair percentage of UK forces as well as many overseas were on Triumph.

Right: Although General de Gaulle was a difficult character and was not over fond of the British he was a tremendous wartime figure and his Free French forces performed valiantly in many theatres of war. Here he is seen taking part in some important occasion escorted by the French gendarmerie on their Triumphs. The rider in the foreground is eyeing the dicey wet cobblestones with intense concentration.

Below: Many will remember the famous Victory Parade photograph of the Metropolitan Police squad passing the saluting base in the Mall; it hung in Reception at Meriden for many years. This picture, not seen before, was taken a few minutes earlier as the police riders passed through Admiralty Arch. The date was 8th June 1946.

Here is another state occasion. This was the Silver Wedding Drive of King George VI and Queen Elizabeth on 26th April 1948, passing along Great Dover Street. You will note how the Triumph - mounted police escort is carefully avoiding the notorious London tramlines. The centre slot for the power pick-up was an additional hazard which caused the downfall of many motorcyclists – I know only too well, I was one of them!

Here we see Emperor Haile Selassie of Ethiopia, on a visit to Tanganyika in 1964 (now known as Tanzania). The official Rolls-Royce has the usual Triumph-mounted escort – and very smart they look too. Not a very dense crowd of spectators, but they do appear to be clapping quite enthusiastically.

I am not sure of the identity of the two obviously important gentlemen standing up in the official car but the bikes are Triumph and the arch in the background is undoubtedly that famous Paris landmark, the Arc de Triumph – sorry Triomphe. Note the security guards keeping a close watch from the top of the arch.

MERIDEN MOMENTS

No 4 THE GAFFER'S GRAND PRIX!

The sleek silver Grand Prix model was standing outside the Triumph Experimental Department at Meriden where two mechanics were giving it a final polish. It had been prepared for a customer who was due at any moment. The GP was popular in the late forties and early fifties with competitors for whom the Manx Norton and Mk VIII Velos were out of reach financially. The GP was never designed to compete seriously with those two classics – it was, after all, only a souped-up Tiger 100. Nevertheless on its day it was no sluggard as victories in the 1946 and 1948 Manx GPs and at Daytona proved.

The mechanics shuffled nervously as the sturdy figure of Edward Turner was seen striding along the front of the factory towards them. They knew he had no love for racing machinery and might start asking awkward questions. He stopped at the GP, ran a keen eye over it, and was told that it was ready for action. To the onlookers' surprise he climbed aboard and the mechanics were commanded to push. The next moment twin megaphones blasted an impossible decibel level outside the offices where startled faces appeared at windows.

Machine and rider motored along the front of the factory, and a blipping throttle increased the appalling cacophony. Suddenly the exhaust cleared as ET took a handful of throttle and headed, not back along the factory but out on to the A45 road. Accelerating violently the machine streaked towards the top of Meriden Hill, its rider crouched over the bars, his trilby hat brim flattened against the crown. Astonished employees totted up the crimes being committed by their MD as the noise faded over the top of the hill. No tax, no insurance, no silencers, no number plates, excessive speed etc. etc. Helmets were not then compulsory or that would have been another one!

Soon the noise could be heard again as the GP howled back down the hill. Rapid downward changes sounded rather like Ernie Lyons approaching Creg-ny-Baa as rider and bike swept through the factory gates. Back along the front of the works, ET's windswept appearance confirmed that he had not been hanging about. Without a word, he handed the GP backed to the mechanics and stalked off to his office on the first floor.

Who said manufacturers never rode their own products?

INTERNATIONAL SIX DAYS TRIAL

One of the big events of the post-war trials scene was the International Six Days Trial (or ISDT for short). As its name implies it was a six day event and was held annually in various European countries with the exception of the 1973 trial which went to the United States.

The rules of the ISDT in no way resembled those applying to one-day trials. There were no observed sections, no loss of marks for footing or stopping – it was decided on a very tight time schedule. Riders had to 'clock in' at numerous check points along the route, so that arriving late lost marks. Each day the route followed a different circuit and the 'roads' were invariably rough, steep and narrow. Mountain tracks climbing skywards tested the machines to the limit and high speeds were essential to meet the schedules set. It was rather like a long distance motocross. Riders needed exceptional stamina as well as considerable technical knowledge to keep their machines going if faults developed. Outside assistance was prohibited and was penalised if detected.

Primarily the trial was a contest between national teams for the 'International Trophy'. One team only per nation was permitted and they had to ride machines manufactured in their own country. The secondary contest, for the 'International Silver Vase' allowed two teams per nation and any make of machine could be used. Apart from these two competitions the event was open to anyone and Gold and Silver Medals could be won. There were team prizes for manufacturers and clubs.

The very first event was held in Great Britain in 1913 in the Lake District, with Carlisle as headquarters. Triumph had seven entries in the 500cc category and all finished, winning five Gold and two Bronze medals. The event restarted in 1920 and Triumph riders were among the award winners every year from then on. In 1948 Triumph began a run of successes which went on for a long time. That year Allan Jefferies was captain of the Trophy-winning British team on a 500cc Triumph twin which later became the famous "Trophy" model – a light, fast and very popular clubman mount which could be used for almost any sort of two wheel activity barring the Isle of Man TT. It achieved great fame in the United States with a 650cc engine – the TR6.

Jim Alves, the factory's No 1 rider in post-war years, was a member of the winning British Vase team in 1948 and with Jefferies and Gaymer won a manufacturer's team award. Alves moved up to the British Trophy team the following year and retained his position in it until 1955. During this time the British team were outright winners in 1948/49/50/51/53, second in 1954 and third in 1952 and 1955. Triumph won manufacturer's team awards in 1948, 1949, 1950, 1951 and 1954.

The successful Triumph teams comprised the following riders:-

1948 – Allan Jefferies, Jim Alves, Bert Gaymer.
1949 – Jim Alves, Bert Gaymer, Bob Manns.
1950/51 – Jim Alves, Bert Gaymer, Peter Hammond.
1954 – Jim Alves, Peter Hammond, John Giles.

Their mounts were 500s mainly but due to a regulation which called for machines in the Trophy teams to be of two different capacities Triumph, after the introduction of the Thunderbird in 1949, were able to replace the 500 engine with a 650, a very simple conversion.

The photographs which follow are a selection taken during International Six Day Trials in various locations but mostly in the UK where photography poses fewer problems than in certain other countries. When held in the UK, Wales was the most favoured area, its mountain passes and forest tracks providing ideal going with an almost complete absence of traffic and spectators. The Isle of Man was also used on two occasions later, in 1965 and 1971.

Allan Jefferies, Captain of the British Trophy Team, sweeps round a very loose bend in the 1948 ISDT, held in Italy. Britain won the Trophy and the Vase, with no marks lost. The Triumph team – Jefferies, Alves and Gaymer – won a Manufacturer's Team Award, also losing no marks.

Bert Gaymer in a hurry in the 1948 event; could be the speed test as he is wearing a helmet. The machines used were 500cc twins based on the Speed Twin but with alloy cylinder barrels. Frames were rigid (swinging arms were still to come) and weight was saved wherever possible.

Bob Manns cornering in the final speed test in the 1949 event, held in Wales. This was at Eppynt and Manns, together with Alves and Gaymer, went on to collect yet another manufacturer's team award for Triumph.

The ever popular Molly Briggs footing along a rough bank in the 1950 trial, which was also held in Wales. This was obviously a popular spot with spectators.

Jim Alves braking briskly with the forks well down. The square alloy barrel from the wartime generator set can be clearly seen. This was used on the first production Trophy models until a more elegant design came along. Photograph from the 1950 trial in Wales where GB won both the Trophy and Vase.

Another shot of Molly in the same event. Here she is motoring confidently along one of the mountain tracks
40 which abound in the Welsh mountains and which make it an ideal venue for the ISDT.

Bert Gaymer in Italy 1951. Helmets were not compulsory except in the speed test and British riders stuck to their old cloth caps, usually worn back to front.

Gaymer again in Italy 1951. Britain won the Trophy with Alves in the team. Triumph picked up another manufacturer's team award, the team being Alves, Gaymer and Hammond.

Overleaf top: Peter Hammond in Italy 1951. He won a Gold, losing no marks. He looks relaxed enough here in the Italian sunshine and with a nice clean bike.

Overleaf bottom: Peter Hammond sweeps through what appears to be a rather unkempt collection of farm buildings in Italy 1951. Could be early in the morning by the absence of spectators – the Italians love a 'race' particularly on their own doorstep.

Italy 1951, Jim Alves on his 650 Triumph being chased by a single cylinder Royal Enfield during the speed test at the Monza circuit. Two different engine capacities were obligatory for the Trophy team hence Jim's 650.

Now we are in Czechoslovakia. They won the Trophy in 1952 so claimed the right to organise the event in 1953. Peter Hammond is extracting himself from a rather unpleasant swamp-like area.

John Giles eases himself onto the rests to tackle a fast uphill section. This was Czechoslovakia 1953, John won a Silver Medal but the Trophy went to Great Britain – beating the Czechs on their home ground!

Another shot of Giles in '53, leading a string of other competitors out of the wood. The days of the flat hat, with peak at the back, seem to be over – it's all helmets now.

Having won the Trophy in 1953 we are now back in Wales for 1954. Jim Alves going well in his usual masterly manner but he's picked up a lot of Welsh mud.

John Giles sweeping round a Welsh mountain hairpin on his way to the next check. He won a Special Gold Medal along with Hammond and Alves but the Czechs snatched the Trophy back – on **our** home ground!

B.H. Olie (650 Triumph), a member of the Dutch Vase "A" Team, showers the riders behind with a few gallons of pure Welsh mountain stream – that's one way of keeping ahead.

F.H. Climpson (500 Triumph) waves a leg, I'm not quite sure why. Maybe the enormous crack in the wall alarmed him. The gentleman on the extreme right with pipe is the late Arthur Bourne, much respected editor of *The Motor Cycle* at that time.

John Giles, a member of the British Vase "B" Team in 1954, checks in at some remote location in wildest Wales. It is actually 5½ miles from Cynghordy according to the signpost, if that's any help.

O. Helander (500 Triumph), a member of the Finnish Vase "A" Team, makes a splash as he heads for higher ground. This was 1954 in Wales. Not much in the way of scenery at this spot.

P. Bogehoj scrambles his 500 Triumph out of the river while other competitors seem to be having problems. What is the lady in the foreground doing, is she trying to snatch the folded up inner tube attached to the rider's shoulder?

S.E. Keepence (250 Triumph) heads a Continental sidecar down a particularly vicious stretch of rockery. How do they manage with the sidecar on the wrong side? Wales 1954.

A particularly good close-up shot of Jim Alves really motoring in Wales. He finished with a clean sheet but Great Britain were 2nd to the Czechs in 1954. Holland won the Vase, we came 3rd. Not a good year for us.

An interesting look at the British camp in 1955 when the trial was held in Czechoslovakia. Jim Alves on the right, Len Heath Team Manager next to him (in sports jacket). On the left, Henry Vale, who for many years prepared all the Triumph works competition machines.

Electrics can be a nightmare to an ISDT competitor and if he wants to finish he must know every wire and connection - and be able to find them under the mud! Here Jim Alves, Trophy Team member, keeps an eye on the man from Lucas who is doing some work on the wiring of his Triumph prior to the trial.

Left: ISDT Wales 1950. Jim Alves receives his route card for the following day. Jim was in the victorious British Trophy Team and the Team Award - winning Triumph works team – his clean performance earning him a Gold – no one could do more.

Right: Bert Gaymer relaxes with Rex Young, another competitor, during the 1951 ISDT at Varese, Italy. The number of nubile young Italian women around might have upset a rider's concentration but Bert still won his Gold!

Edward Turner paid a flying visit to the 1954 ISDT in Wales. With him is Bill Johnson, West Coast (USA) distributor for Triumph and good friend of ET since pre-war days. Henry Vale, who prepared the bikes, hides modestly between the two. The rider, Peter Hammond, went on to win a Gold.

Another Army entrant in 1961 reports to his 'boss'. Engine running, clutch out, front brake on – "Don't keep me talking too long, I'm due out in 30 seconds".

Opposite top: The 1961 trial was won by Germany and the event moved to Germany for 1962. After that it went to Czechoslovakia (1963), Germany (1964), Isle of Man (1965), Sweden (1966), Poland (1967), Italy (1968), Germany (1969), Spain (1970) Isle of Man (1971), Czechoslovakia (1972) and the USA (1973). This is a convenient spot to finish our story with a photograph of the British Trophy team for the American event:-

They are (L to R) Ken Heanes, Manager, 79 Jim Sandiford (125 Rickman), 297 John Pease (504 Triumph), 269 Alan Lampkin (500 Triumph), 289 Arthur Browning (504 Triumph), 252 Malcolm Rathmell (500 Triumph), 42 Ernie Page (125 Rickman).

The trial was held in the Berkshire area of Massachusetts, in the north eastern corner of the USA. It is mountainous with a lot of damp and deep forests where the sun rarely filters through. With these murky conditions in mind Ken Heanes made sure that special attention was paid to waterproofing the bikes used by the Trophy team. The finish for the Trophy was a close one, Czechoslovakia winning with no marks lost. Great Britain came second with a loss of just 4 marks. All our riders with the exception of Arthur Browning won Golds; Arthur's reward was a Silver after he was delayed when five of the eight bolts holding his rear sprocket sheared. The American "A" team won the Silver Vase on Husqvarna machines losing 8 marks, Sweden "A" was second with 23 marks lost.

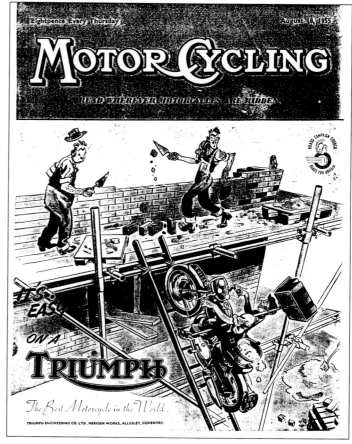

THE 1973 ISDT TRIUMPH

These photographs show very clearly what is needed in the design and preparation of a competitive machine for the ISDT. Every possible cause of failure is worked out and modifications made to cope quickly with it should the worst happen. Wheels come out easily, electrics are duplicated so that a new unit can be plugged into the circuit in seconds. Chains can be adjusted quickly and accurately and so on. Four Triumph TR5Ts were included in the British Trophy Team for the 1973 ISDT in America (two 500cc, two 504cc to comply with the regs) and they won three Gold Medals and one Silver.

Left: Offside view of TR5T model, this photograph shows:-
(a) Cover over electrical system. (b) Lightweight plastic guards. (c) "Bator" forks. (d) Rickman QD front wheel. (e) QD wheel spindles. (f) B50MX seat with zip fasteners to enable tools to be carried inside. (g) Leather tool bag to carry spare chains, etc. (h) Rear chain adjustment. (i) Reinforced plastic number plates. (j) Large alloy plate undershield. (k) 250 BSA/Triumph QD rear wheel modified to fit TR5T swinging arm.**531**

Left bottom: Nearside view of TR5T ISDT model showing:- (a) Rear brake pedal over footrest. (b) Propstand. (c) Remote mounted plastic front guard. (d) Rickman QD front wheel with 6 inch brake. (e) 250 BSA/Triumph QD rear wheel modified to fit TR5T swinging arm. (f) Leather cover over air cleaner.

(a) Footbrake pedal reshaped over folding footrest to avoid trapping on ground on application. (b) Special air cleaner box enclosed in leather cover edged with 'Velcro' and held by studs. (c) L/H end of notched snail cam with 12 notches giving $\frac{3}{4}$ inch movement to adjust rear chain. (d) Tube welded to lower frame tube to protect chaincase.

(a) Electrical system all mounted on offside under leather cover held with 'Velcro' and studs. (b) Quickly adjusted rear chain. Undo large nut and turn spindle with ½ inch A/F ring spanner. Snail cams move in unison so retaining chain alignment. (c) Emergency electrical changeovers – 3 coils – centre one c/w lead, changeover wires only to isolate failed parts. 2 capacitors – 2 rectifiers – 2 zener diodes. (d) Burgess pattern silencer fed by two exhaust pipes joined under gearbox. (e) Simplified electrical wiring – no battery or switch and direct lighting.

Opposite top: (a) Front forks fitted in USA. Light alloy lugs and pull out front wheel spindle. (b) Centre mounted speedometer (rubber mounted). (c) Headlamp fixings on rubber bushes. (d) Plastic racing number plate/integral with front number plate made to comply with regulations. (e) Plastic front guard, remotely mounted on lightweight bracket with rubber inserts. (f) Junction box for QD throttle cable can be seen in front of frame oil tank filler cap.

Opposite bottom: Top view of machine showing:- (a) Alloy tank with single bolt centre fixing. (b) Oil filler cap in front of petrol tank. (c) QD throttle arrangement. Junction box in centre of bars. 2 cables taped together and Magura twistgrip modified for instant cable removal. Spring dirt cover. (d) Central rubber-mounted speedometer. (e) Plastic covers on levers.

The immense amount of work and thought that went into these machines paid off in the results. Tribute must go to Henry Vale assisted by Vic Fidler who were responsible for the preparation of Meriden's competition bikes for many years. Not only did they build and prepare the machines but Henry Vale went with them on their trips abroad to help deal with any mechanical problems. This did not happen very often as the number of Gold Medals and Team Awards won by our riders proves.

ISDT MANUFACTURER'S TEAM AWARD MEDALS

This is what they rode for! A small selection of medals won by the Triumph teams, mounted on an 'all-action' photographic background by John Davies.

(Far left) Italy 1948

(Left) Wales 1950

(Top centre) Germany 1936

(Bottom centre) Wales 1949

(Right) Wales 1954

(Far right) Italy 1951

Below: Reverse views much enlarged, showing inscriptions.

Italy 1948

Wales 1949

Wales 1950

MERIDEN MOMENTS
No 5 FAMOUS LAST WORDS

Triumph policy towards racing was well known. If standard machines, suitable fettled, could be used then Edward Turner was prepared to match Triumph against anything. To build special racers which bore no resemblance to the showroom product, using scarce cash and the company's best brains, was commercial suicide, in his opinion. He would often list companies which had done this and had gone to the wall. Despite this official attitude there were many keen racing enthusiasts at Meriden, some of whom were employed in that holy of holies, the experimental department.

One day, a young man from New Zealand arrived at the works. He had entered himself in the Senior TT and was looking for a bike and maybe some help. Officially this was not on, but there just happened to be this rather wicked looking Tiger 100 tucked away in a corner under wraps, on which a lot of work had been done after closing time by the abovementioned keen types. Oddly enough it looked just like an IOM racer and this appeared to be a heaven-sent opportunity for the bike to show its paces without the management being any the wiser. Who would suspect any connection with someone from as far away as New Zealand? So after a quick check over, the bike was despatched post haste to the Island.

Turner usually went to the TT where he could enjoy himself, happy in the thought that Triumph money was not being poured down the TT drain, whilst that of some of his competitors most certainly was. Strolling behind the pits one day his keen eye caught this impressive looking racer with the familiar Triumph logo on the tank. The mechanic sitting on it in the sunshine seemed familiar too. "Whose is this?" he asked. The reply was a classic example of famous last words – "It's ours, sir," said the lad, with a ring of pride in his voice.

GAFFERS GALLOP

This title was coined by *Motor Cycling* when reporting a very unusual event that took place from 5th to 10th October 1953. It was Turner's idea in the first place needless to say – I don't think anyone else would have dared to suggest it! The plot was for Turner, Bob Fearon (Works Director) and Alec Masters (Service Manager) to ride three Terriers from Land's End to John O'Groats in an attempt to (I quote) "demonstrate the reliability and economy of the 150cc ohv Triumph Terrier". The Terrier had just been announced and this quotation is from the official and very detailed schedule which I still have.

In addition to going from L.E. to J.O'G. extra mileage was covered in order to bring the total up to 1000, 1010 to be exact. The photograph shows the happy middle-aged trio before starting – they were still smiling at the end and claimed to have enjoyed every minute.

They certainly achieved their target as the average speed overall worked out at 36.68 mph and petrol consumption was 108.60 mpg.

MERIDEN MOMENTS
No 6 DESERT SONG

This story is not strictly a 'Meriden' moment but concerns a Meriden product, the Tina scooter, a cunning little vehicle with infinitely variable transmission which ensured that you were always in the right ratio at the right time (or most of it).

Now the trouble with most British lightweights, and the Tina was no exception, was that in order to be competitive, pennies had to be saved and some of the components were not quite as robust as they might have been and this showed up on the road in dubious reliability.

My story concerns a scooter sold to a lady in a Middle Eastern country (which shall be nameless) by an eminently trustworthy

dealer (whose name I have forgotten). It is a true story, because I was there just after it happened. So many times did this poor scooter stop at the roadside that the dealer, called upon to retrieve it each time, became somewhat disenchanted. So much so that one day his breakdown team picked up the Tina, proceeded on into the desert and deposited it there. A phone call to the worried owner inferred that the scooter was not where she had indicated and in all probability it had been stolen – what bad luck!

MERIDEN MOMENTS
No 7 CONVERSATION PIECE

The two Triumph engineers had been on the receiving end of our Managing Director's invective for something like an hour or more and were cheesed off to say the least. Turner on a bad day was a daunting prospect and this was a *BAD* day.

Nothing could satisfy the man, so in the end the two men gave up and devised a conspiracy of silence (neither were very garrulous at the best of times incidentally). They offered no suggestions, no comments, no excuses, nothing – just stood there listening. In the end the big man could stand it no longer: "For God's sake one of you grunt, if only to indicate that a conversation is in progress," he roared.

THUNDERBIRDS OVER MONTLHERY

The story of the Thunderbird demonstration at Montlhéry in 1949 has been told many times and I am going to tell it again here, briefly, but before going into detail it is worth looking at the significance of this event in the world-wide motorcycling picture.

Up to this time your average sporting motorcyclist would be found on a 500 because this category had been highly developed over many years and there was a wide choice. Ariel, AJS, BSA, Matchless, Norton, Panther, Royal Enfield, Rudge, Scott, Sunbeam, Triumph, Velocette and Vincent HRD are some of the names, British, proven and popular in all parts of the world.

There had always been machines with engines bigger than 500cc but, apart from being more expensive, they were not popular and we can thank racing for this. Top capacity for solo road racing had always been 500cc and factories had spent more time and money extracting maximum performance from their 500cc engines than from any others and these were the ones that sold.

Now the 500cc Triumph Speed Twin introduced in 1938 owed nothing to racing but such was its performance (at the right price) that it set a new trend which altered the course of motorcycle design everywhere. Twins were 'in', singles were 'out'. However, after the war the renaissance of the American market, which had been assiduously cultivated by Edward Turner ever since 1937, began to affect marketing decisions in the UK. The Americans wanted even more performance. For Triumph this was a relatively simple matter. The 500cc Speed Twin engine was uprated to 650cc by a simple bore and stroke operation which produced an additional 7 bhp. This entailed no alteration to the motorcycle itself and any extra costs were negligible. A higher price could be charged though, which was good for profits.

The significance of the Thunderbird was that it broke the 500cc 'stranglehold' and paved the way for the introduction of the so-called 'Superbike' developed to the ultimate by the Japanese with their multi cylinder 750s, 1000s and above. Whether this was a good thing or not is open to debate.

Back to the Thunderbird in September 1949. We wanted to make a really memorable model launch and many were the debates in Turner's office and elsewhere on this subject. It had to be a high speed

A re-fuelling stop for Machine No 2 with Alex Scobie in the saddle. Tyrell Smith looks after the oil while Allan Jefferies tops up the tank. Scobie's job at Meriden was high speed long distance testing – a job we would all love to do, except when it was raining – Alex never seemed to notice!

demonstration of some kind and in the end it was decided to attempt 500 miles at 90 mph, not with one model but with three. Tyrell Smith and Ernie Nott in Experimental reckoned, after long testing, that this could be done so we decided to have a go.

Brooklands was no longer useable so we had to go to the Montlhéry circuit near Paris. The riders were recruited from our works trials riders and testers – they were Jim Alves, Bob Manns, Allan Jefferies, Alex Scobie and Len Bayliss. Neale Shilton, Sales Manager, was in charge of all arrangements and 'admin' and he rode one of the machines to France. All these riders were used to high speed but not on a concrete circuit. To prove that the models were genuine production models and not 'specials' they were to be ridden to the circuit and back again afterwards. The day of the 7 litre Motorhome and fleet of back-up vehicles

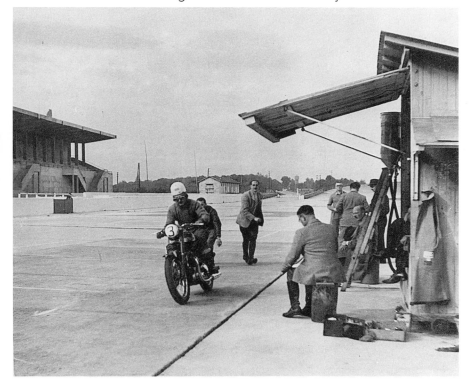

was a long way off! The ACU was enlisted to ensure fair play and their representative was the celebrated one-legged sidecar driver Harold Taylor. The press would be present in the persons of Bob Holliday *(Motor Cycling)* and George Wilson *(The Motor Cycle)*.

To cut a long story short the performances recorded (allowing for stops) were as follows:- No 1 Machine 92.23 mph, No 2 Machine 92.48 mph, No 3 Machine 92.33 mph for the 500 miles. They then covered single laps of the circuit at 100.71, 101.78 and 100.71 mph respectively. After this they were ridden back to Coventry where Harold Taylor carried out an inspection which involved stripping the engines and to quote a press report afterwards, all three machines "looked capable of an immediate repeat performance".

Jim Alves takes off from the 'pit' on No 3 Machine. Jim was our No 1 trials rider and has an impressive collection of Gold Medals from the International Six Days Trial in which he was a member of the British Trophy Team for many years. He found the concrete rather different from the rough stuff he was used to but his rides were right up to the schedule specified.

MERIDEN MOMENTS

No 8 TURNER TURNS TOO TIGHTLY

Leading off the A45 road into the Triumph works there was a short approach road from which one turned sharp right along the front of the factory to the offices at the far end.

Due to the fact that so many drivers cut across the corner damaging the lawn, a series of stout iron posts about 2 feet high were inserted round the edge of the bend to discourage this practice.

One day Managing Director Edward Turner, always in a hurry, always impatient, swept in at speed in his big Armstrong Siddeley 'Sapphire'. He cut the corner all right, despite the posts, which proceeded to inflict an interesting redesign on the offside of his car. It finished up with a line of artistically arranged waves down half its length.

Looking at this damage later in the day, Works Director Alf Camwell scratched his head and said, "You'd have a helluva job to design a tool to get that shape into production."

WORLD TRAVELLERS

World Travellers on two wheels – what can I say about them? To go round the world on a motorcycle is not exactly the easiest or most comfortable way of doing it, a Jumbo would be preferable! Nevertheless there was never any shortage of enthusiasts who were determined to try. Not many succeeded. A lot of courage, a lot of guts and immense self-confidence are needed to be a Ted Simon or Paul Pratt. The bike has to be reliable too and you have to know what to do when it is not. Everything you are likely to need both for man and beast has to be carried either on the beast or on you. The resulting Christmas tree effect does not make riding the bike any easier.

Yet some have done it and I take off my hat to them; the spirit of Drake and Raleigh is still alive and well!

ANTHONY SMITH, BBC broadcaster, balloonist, adventurer at large bought a second-hand Tiger Cub in Cape Town in 1955 and rode it home. 28 years later, riding the same Tiger Cub and accompanied by his 19 year old son, Adam, on another Cub. He reversed the operation and rode from Egypt to South Africa via the Sudan, Uganda, Kenya, Tanzania, Zambia and Zimbabwe, also taking in Swaziland. The Cubs, of 1954 and 1963 vintage, were prepared by Hughie Hancox, the well-known Coventry restorer and ex-factory service engineer.

Right: Anthony Smith with his Cub, the one that carried him from Cape Town to England in 1955.

Adam Smith with both bikes at the South Africa/Swaziland border.

A spot of clutch bother en route – nothing serious and quickly rectified after the plates were rearranged.

The work force who fixed the bikes in Nairobi and who actually owned three Cubs between them.

Adam Smith on the roadside between Alexandria and Cairo, their first resting point in Africa. Not much in the way of scenery! His father's Cub can be seen in the background.

The Smith's washing line complete with helmets, after arrival in Cape Town. The famous Table Mountain can be seen in the background.

TED SIMON

As I have said elsewhere would-be world travellers on motorcycles were a pain to busy factories and had to be discouraged courteously but firmly. The letter I received on the heading of a national Sunday paper was something different. Its writer was Ted Simon who, on interview, impressed sufficiently to make me think twice about his project. In the end he got his bike, an ex-police 500 I believe it was. After some intensive riding practice in France and sessions in the factory Repair Shop on maintenance, he hung all his gear on the bike and set off, looking rather like a mobile Christmas tree.

Ted Simon and his trusty steed snapped in Brazil.

Opposite top: Ted out in the wilds somewhere; you see what I meant by the bike looking like a Christmas tree.

Opposite: Ted Simon in close-up; he could just be saying "It's easy on a Triumph".

Four years or so later he arrived back, having gone just about all round the world. From England he headed south through France, Italy, Libya, Egypt then right down to South Africa. From there to Brazil. Argentina, Bolivia and Peru followed, then up to Mexico and California. By sea again to New Zealand via Hawaii then to Australia. Across Australia thence to Malaysia, India and Tibet, from where he headed west for home via Iran, Turkey, Yugoslavia, Switzerland and France. I don't guarantee the accuracy of this route, the map in Ted's book Jupiter's Travels is a very small scale one.

There were a few problems he ran into which the factory or its distributors overseas managed to cope with but in general the bike performed well and can be seen today in the Motor Museum in Coventry. Total road mileage was 60,647 and sea rail or ferry trips came to 17,655 miles. Quite a journey!

PAUL PRATT

Paul Pratt was an interesting character whose world travels became a way of life. He might have got round the world eventually but he seemed to move from place to place staying days, weeks or months in each as the fancy took him. He earned a little money or maybe a roof over his head by giving talks and lectures to the locals. His means of transport was a Thunderbird which from time to time misbehaved slightly, which prompted Paul to write the longest letters you've ever seen to me, to the Service Manager, to the Spares Manager and to anyone else he could think of at the factory. We all groaned when we saw them but managed, between us, to keep him moderately happy and mobile. In between trips he turned up at the works with his bike and we did what we could for him and sent him on his way. He had a slightly exaggerated idea of the value of the publicity he thought he was creating round the world but he meant well and was a great Triumph enthusiast.

Paul Pratt in the wilds somewhere with his Thunderbird and two little lady friends.

Mr A.E. CATT

I make no excuse for showing this picture of Mr Catt again (it was in that other book) simply to demonstrate here among the modern examples that monstrous long rides are nothing new in the motorcycle world. Mr Catt belongs to those halcyon days before the First World War and was the proud owner of a 3½ hp Triumph free engine model with ball bearing magneto ignition. On this he became the holder of the ''Six Consecutive Days Record All England Route'' covering 2,557 miles and averaging 426 miles a day. This was in May 1911.

Mr A.E. Catt with his 3½ hp Triumph.

UNUSUAL PHOTOGRAPHS

Some unusual but interesting pictures from my collection. I am not quite sure where some of them came from but suspect the BSA Public Relations Department. They loved to put out pictures like this – particularly the one of Karen Gardner on the M1.

During a visit to Australia some years ago Lord Snowdon acquired a Bonneville and is here seen enjoying a dice with a couple of friends on the track outside Perth. He has also sampled the TT course in the Isle of Man. His Tiger 100, which he kept in London, was serviced by Meriden from time to time.

Posing this picture on a bridge over the M1 in 1961 nearly caused several nasty accidents as truck drivers' attention was diverted from the road to this well-developed young lady – one Karen Gardner, our favourite model. The other model looks like a T100S/S of the following year.

Another very brief comment "Les Hirondelles, Paris". Lovely vintage 'traction avant' Citroën, shades of Rupert Davies as Maigret, the French TV 'tec. Bikes are Triumph.

The inscription on this print simply says –"Austrian acrobats using 1952 Triumph Terrier". Sooner them than me!

Bottom: With their menacing Lightning fighters in the background what are the pilots doing wasting their time riding around on Tina scooters? The idea was to provide pilot transport on the airfield but nothing came of it.

Below: Now we have cyclists in a motorcycle book – what goes on? The occasion is the 1952 Sports Day at the Triumph factory and the rider with the hat is none other than H.G. Tyrell Smith, winner of the 1930 Junior TT, who is about to win the Slow Bicycle Race! Tyrell was head of Experimental at the time.

And what is this car doing here? Firstly it is a Triumph. Secondly it has some achievements to its name like most of the bikes in this book. Thirdly it dates back to the thirties when Triumph cars, motorcycles, sidecars and bicycles were all made in the Priory Street works in Coventry where this photograph was taken. The poster on the showroom window reads – "Triumph Gloria Wins Monte Carlo Rally, Light Car Class. Best Performance of any British Car. 7 Triumph Glorias Started, 7 Triumph Glorias Finished etc, etc" So it was "Easy on a Triumph" even in those days – and with four wheels too!

No 9 THE CHEQUE THAT NEVER CAME

This little story has nothing to do with Triumph motorcycles but it did happen at Meriden and it did concern Edward Turner. It was in 1959 and he had just designed two vee - eight engines of $2\frac{1}{2}$ and $4\frac{1}{2}$ litres, to replace the ageing units in the Daimler range of cars for which he had recently become responsible. The smaller engine went initially into a brand new two-seater sports car, the SP 250, which had a fibreglass body.

This was launched at the New York Motor Show in 1959 and as the idea of a Daimler sports car was quite unprecedented, Turner was invited by the prestigious London *Financial Times* to submit an article entitled

'The British Sports Car' during the course of which he would be able to promote his new baby. It was to fill a whole page of this large format newspaper and there was room for several photographs. He threw it at me and said, "Have a go at this, and they want it by the end of the week" or words to that effect.

My knowledge of sports cars, British or otherwise, was strictly limited but I did some research, found a few suitable photographs and produced a reasonable story of about 2000 words which I gave to the boss. He read it, grunted, and sent it off. It duly appeared in the paper on 19th October 1959 with "Edward Turner, M.I.Mech.E. Managing Director B.S.A. Automotive Division" in bold capitals at the top. It appeared exactly as I had written it, he had not altered so much as a comma!

The sequel occurred 25 years later and I can relate this now that the principal figures, ET and his secretary Nan Plant, have, sadly, passed on. I was talking to Nan one day when she recalled this article and said that Turner had received a cheque for it from the paper. She had asked him if she should pass it on to me and the reply was – "No I don't think so, **it would only set a precedent"**.

SCRAMBLING

Off-road races were always known as 'scrambles' in the period covered by this book and to ride in them was to go 'scrambling'. Today the sport is called 'motocross'. Why we should adopt a foreign word in place of a perfectly good English one I do not know. I prefer 'scrambling' and offer some photographs of well-known Triumph-mounted scramblers from the not too distant past. This was a rugged sport and called for great physical effort on the part of the rider and robustness on the part of the motorcycle. There were not many of today's lightweight two-strokes around, the bikes used were big 500s and 650s and these took some handling, but on a fast course they were very spectacular.

This is the earliest photograph that I have in my files of Jim Alves. He started riding seriously after the war on a Velo but this picture shows him on an ex-WD 350 Triumph 3HW. This model, developed from the pre-war 3H, handled well and had a fair performance. I do not doubt that Jim made a Tiger 80 of it! The event is the Dartmoor Open Scramble, 8th August 1947, and the winner was P.H. Alves (Triumph)! This was before the works recognised his talents and signed him up.

Bob Manns was a tester at the factory and had the ability, which many testers did not have, of being able to pinpoint not just the malfunction in the bike he was testing but the reason for it. He was also a top class competition rider and was in the works team for several years. Here he is obviously trying very hard in a local Coventry event, the Binley Scramble of 1949. **1002**

Below: Ken Heanes going well in a scramble at Golding Barn, Small Dole near Shoreham, Sussex, sometime in the mid-fifties. He is being chased hard by Ron Stillo on another 500 Triumph. **1003**

Right: A shot of the redoubtable Gordon Blakeway on his 500 Triumph.

Another shot of Gordon Blakeway. You will note he is attired in a natty sports jacket and open neck shirt! He is being chased by none other than World Champion Jeff Smith (No 4).

John Giles at speed, place and date unknown. For some reason he is looking rather apprehensive which was unusual for John who was the most cheerful character you could ever wish to meet, whatever the circumstances. A member of the factory team for many years John was equally at home on a sticky trials section, when scrambling or slogging it out in one of the big six day events.

Opposite page: Two from America. The first is described as a "typical sand trap" – the riders being T. Woodward (500 Indian) and Sal Scripi (500 Triumph). The lad on the Indian seems to be heading for disaster with both feet waving in the air whilst the Triumph man is obviously finding it "easy"!

TRIALS

The trials scene has changed quite dramatically in recent times. The advent of the very powerful lightweight two-stroke has completely eliminated the 250, 350 and 500cc four-strokes of the past. These are only used nowadays in events staged especially for them and what a joy it is to hear the "bark of a well tuned single" again. The old timers refer to the modern trials irons as "Mickey Mouse bikes" but concede that when it comes to tackling a tough section, the 'Mickeys' have it every time.

Right: A famous picture of Allan Jefferies on a 500cc side-valve Triumph climbing Breakheart Hill in the 1938 British Experts Trial – which he won! Built more or less for fun the side valver proved remarkably effective.

What they can do is quite astonishing and to see a rider stop dead, feet up, and then lift the front of his bike round sideways in a series of jumps, still feet up, so that it finishes up pointing the way he wants to go next, is a new ball game altogether! Suspensions have changed completely and it is quite normal to have 10 to 12 inches of movement back and front where we had to be satisfied with about $3\frac{1}{2}$ inches. This vast amount of movement results in two things – 1) The ability to surmount the most formidable obstructions in the shape of rocks or tree trunks and 2) The ugliest motorcycles ever seen anywhere.

There are no 'Mickey Mouse' bikes in the following photographs, Triumph never made anything like that – perhaps we should have done but Edward Turner's eye for appearance and shape would never have tolerated it. I can well imagine his comments confronted with one of today's trials models!!

1939 Land's End Trial. The author on his Tiger 80 maintained a clean sheet and has an engraved clock from the MCC to prove it.

Above: Jim Alves on the little 350 twin in the 1946 West of England Trial. The usual black tank has been swapped for a tank in Tiger colours.

Above right: Peter Hammond working hard on what appears to be a fairly smooth patch. This was the era when the 350 twin was making a name for itself in trials circles.

Jim Alves working his 500 through a tricky section in the 1952 Hurst Cup Trial.

Jack Wicken also in the Hurst Cup Trial but two years later.

Jim Alves was one of the first works riders to go over to a lightweight – a 150cc Terrier, here seen in the 1954 Cotswold Cups Trial. Later the 200cc Cubs were used. Today, nothing but lightweights are to be seen.

Opposite top: Jim Alves again, this time threading his way through a snowy section in the 1954 Colmore Cup Trial on his Terrier.

Opposite bottom: Peter Hammond in trouble on his Cub. The back wheel seems to have a mind of its own and wants to go down the bank. A shot from the late fifties.

Following pages:
A superb shot of Ray Sayer on Loch Eild Path in the Scottish. Intense concentration on the faces of the rider and the spectators. What a view at the back!

This splendid picture of John Giles on a 500 appeared in a foreign journal, location and event unknown. He is riding a 500 in his usual masterly manner.

Artie Ratcliffe sampling a new 500 trials model using swinging arm rear suspension for the first time. This was in 1954.

Right: Jim Alves wrestles with his 500 in what appears to be a sea of mud. He still has his feet firmly on the rests though!

John Giles trickles his Cub through a nasty section on the throttle and eyes the loose rocks ahead.

This picture from the USA is labelled "Traffic Problem - Indian sidecar, BSA 250, Triumph 6T, Pair of Matchlesses, dead NSU, Indian". What it is or where it is I do not know but there is an awful lot of damage being done to those submerged engines.

Another one from the USA, the Jack Pine Run of 1959. These competitors seem to have given up running – for Jack Pine or anyone else. Let's hope the winners are on Triumphs.

Now to Belgium. Joseph Decat, Triumph distributor, battles his Cub past the "Section Ends" card. Decat was very active in the post-war period, both selling Triumphs and riding them.

No 10 'NOTTY' AND THE SUNBEAM

The Sunbeam S7 caused a sensation when it was announced by BSA shortly after the war. It was a 500cc ohc parallel twin with engine-clutch-4 speed-gearbox unit disposed longitudinally in a duplex crable frame with shaft drive to an underslung worm and wheel assembly enclosed in a massive alloy case.

Shortly after its announcement, the one and only Charles Markham, Midlands Editor of *Motor Cycling* arrived at Meriden on an S7, which caused something of a stir! He was roadtesting it for his magazine and thought we might like to have a look at it. We certainly did and it was not long before someone suggested that we ought to have a ride on it. Charley agreed and

we queued up. Soon it was the great Ernie Nott's turn. Ernie, one time Rudge ace, was then a member of the Triumph experimental staff and he motored off up the road to the village and was soon out of sight.

Notty will sort it out we thought and eagerly awaited his return. Nothing happened – five minutes, ten minutes, quarter of an hour – no Notty. Suddenly we saw him coming very slowly down the hill towards the works, not at all in the usual style of "the greatest TT rider never to have won a TT". He turned in to the works and pottered along the front towards the experimental shop at about 5 mph. Something was obviously wrong and that something, inexplicably, turned out to be a broken frame. Markham's face was a picture! He visualised having to explain to the BSA people how their 'friends' at Meriden had broken their precious bicycle. Then the experimental boys went into action! In a very short space of time the broken frame was welded up, resprayed and was as good as new again.

Markham rode away towards Birmingham with relief written all over his face – we doubt whether Small Heath ever found out.

Above left: Decat again in a very artistically arranged shot, this time on a 500 in very snowy conditions. Would make a good Christmas card.

Above: Over to Finland in 1962. This was the newest member of the local Triumph team, Gustaf Ekland, who was leading the Finnish Championship at that time.

EDWARD TURNER

I would like to finish this book with a few comments about the man who brought Triumph to life again in 1936 and launched it into a period of progress and profit the like of which had never been seen before in the British motorcycle industry.

Born in 1901 Turner moved to the Midlands in 1927 and joined the Ariel company which had been acquired by Jack Sangster whose family had been connected with Ariel for many years. The partnership between Turner and Sangster was to last for close on 40 years and its effect on the motorcycle industries of the world was profound. Turner became Technical Director and subsequently Managing Director of Ariel. It was here that he designed the remarkable Ariel Square Four and experimented with the 500cc version, removing the front crankshaft and modifying the rear crankshaft to make what was in effect a 250cc vertical twin. The success of this experiment led to the design of the Speed Twin at Triumph after Turner took charge there in 1936. Triumph was on the point of going out of business at this time but Sangster stepped in, bought it, and put Turner in charge.

The Speed Twin was announced in the 1938 programme and was an instant success. A sporting version, the Tiger 100, followed in 1939 and Triumph was on its way! The all-red vertical twin started a world trend once the war was out of the way. British manufacturers all produced their versions and Oriental and European makers were not far behind.

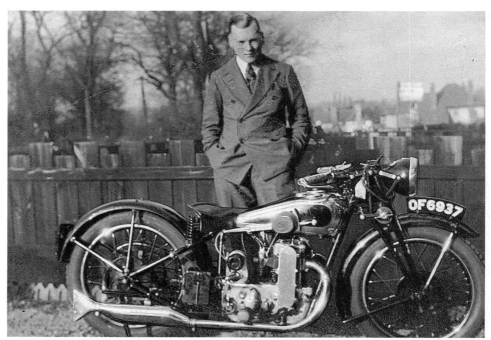

Right: Edward Turner with his first Ariel Square Four. It was on this engine that Turner experimented to convince himself that a vertical twin was a practicable proposition and the Triumph Speed Twin was the result.

The Triumph twin engine was an incredible unit – simple in conception, cheap and easy to make, reliable and very fast. It has satisfied the requirements of hundreds of thousands of owners world-wide. It has won races in the Isle of Man and on many other circuits. Drag strips have echoed to the Triumph snarl where units are often coupled in pairs. It has held the motorcycle World Speed Record on more than one occasion at speeds approaching 250 mph.

During World War II it powered a generator for the RAF. It has been seen in speed boats and racing cars and on one occasion nearly took to the air in a one-man helicopter. All this, yet it started life on Edward Turner's drawing board in Coventry as the power unit for a bread-and-butter sporting motorcycle produced at a strictly competitive price!

Edward Turner was a dynamic and forceful character but he had a very short temper and at times was quite impossible to deal with. However the storms soon blew over and were never resurrected. When in benevolent mood his eloquence was Churchillian both in content and delivery. On these occasions he was most entertaining and whatever the subject his views were forthright and usually provocative. Certain authors have been very critical of him, downright rude in fact, but they didn't know him like those of us who worked with him for 25 years or more.

The success of the company is the yardstick by which he should be judged and no one could argue about that. He picked a good team which stayed together for a long time and he inspired great loyalty in this team one of whom said to me recently:-

"Throughout those halcyon years we learned that the creation, manufacture, advertising and marketing of motorcycles was supporting a young man's game which kept us all at Triumph, more or less broke, but young at heart."

We still meet, we still reminisce over a drink, we still help each other. Some occasionally still ride those gorgeous twins that Edward Turner designed.

I remember walking round the stand at the 1972 Earls Court Show with Turner and his comments on the exhibits were as biting and analytical as ever, despite the fact that his health had obviously deteriorated due to diabetes. He died peacefully at his home in Surrey on 15th August 1973.

Yes, he was a tough character but he had his softer moments. I received this note from him dated 26th February 1948:-

"Dear Davies, Please accept this cheque, with which I hope you will buy a present on the occasion of your marriage. Wishing you a lifetime of happiness, Yours sincerely, Edward Turner".

Triumph at Meriden was an unusual organisation with an unusual bunch of people running it. Turner once said to us:-

"We at Triumph may be a home-spun lot but remember this - in the kingdom of the blind the one-eyed man is King!"

Some of these photographs of Edward Turner have been seen before but the supply is finite - and they are worth showing again in my opinion.

Alongside his favourite drawing board. A photograph by Donald Page, Val Page's son, who was a very popular photographer in our industry at that time.

Edward Turner and Val Page who moved in turn from Ariel to Triumph and created some superb ranges of motorcycles for both companies.

At a company function, the Lord Mayor of Coventry is instructed in the mysteries of a restored 1938 Speed Twin by the man who designed it. **Right:** The "Big Three" who built the Triumph American market up from virtually nothing to the point where it was absorbing most of Meriden's output. (L to R) Denis McCormack, President Triumph Corporation, Baltimore, Bill Johnson, President Johnson Motors Inc. Pasadena, California, and Edward Turner. The United States was divided roughly into half – Denis McCormack handling the eastern half and Bill Johnson the west. *Photo: Jack Cansler.*

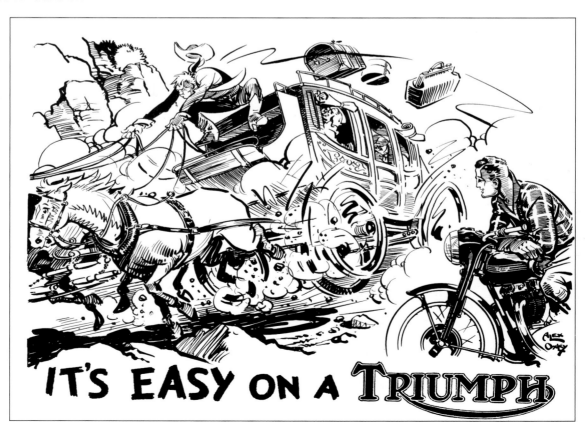